CW00953048

BRANCH LINE TO KINGSBRIDGE

Vic Mitchell and Keith Smith

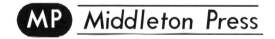

MP Middleton Press

Cover picture: Being refreshed at Kingsbridge on 16th August 1958 is 2-6-2T no. 5533. The water is coming from the tank near the engine shed, both of which are evident on the right. (E.Wilmshurst)

Published November 2002

ISBN 1 901706 98 2

© Middleton Press, 2002

Design   David Pede
Typesetting   Barbara Mitchell

Published by
            Middleton Press
            Easebourne Lane
            Midhurst, West Sussex
            GU29 9AZ
Tel: 01730 813169
Fax: 01730 812601

Printed & bound by Biddles Ltd,
            Guildford and Kings Lynn

INDEX

I. Route diagram from the 1947 Railway Clearing House map.

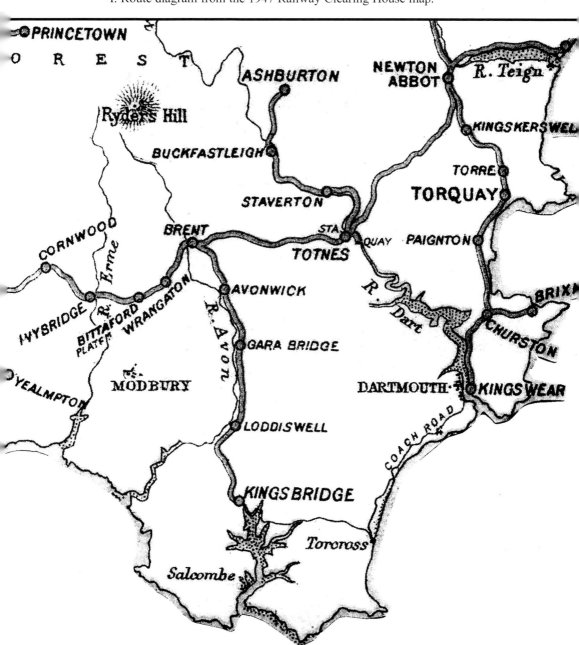

ACKNOWLEDGEMENTS

We are particularly grateful for the input of local knowledge by Mr Ken Williams. As with other albums, we are very appreciative of the assistance given by many of the photographic contributors and also that provided by A.E.Bennett, R.M.Casserley, G.Croughton, Mrs S.Grove, N.Langridge, Mr. D. & Dr. S.Salter, J.J.Smith and our very supportive wives.

GEOGRAPHICAL SETTING

Most of the route follows the south flowing River Avon, which is in a deep valley cut into Red Sandstone. However, the first mile or so is on higher ground, as are the final two. The latter length includes a tunnel at Sorley before the line descends steeply to the terminus on the western border of the historic waterfront town of Kingsbridge, which is five miles from open sea. The area is known as The South Hams.

The maps are to the scale of 25 ins to 1 mile, unless otherwise stated.

HISTORICAL BACKGROUND

The main line was opened by the South Devon Railway on 5th May 1848, it becoming part of the Great Western Railway in 1876.

The branch was authorised by an Act of 25th July 1864, but only four miles of earthworks were completed before financial problems arose. A new company was formed on 24th July 1882, with the optimistic title of the Kingsbridge & Salcombe Railway Co. Ltd.

The line was completed to Kingsbridge only and opened on 19th December 1893, the company having been absorbed by the GWR ten years earlier. Nationalisation in 1948 brought few changes, the route becoming part of the Western Region of British Railways. Traffic continued to diminish and both freight and passenger services ceased on 16th September 1963, although Brent remained open for a further year.

←——————— II. 1946 edition at 1ins to 1 mile.

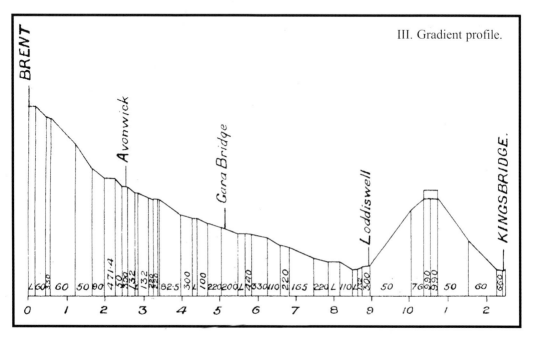

III. Gradient profile.

PASSENGER SERVICES

Few lines have had such a consistent service as this one, there being six down weekday trains in almost every year. One returned empty for long periods.

A through train to and from London on Summer Saturdays was a feature of the timetables from 1950 to 1963, with some prior to World War II. In 1937, they included a restaurant car.

There were sometimes additional journeys on Wednesdays and Saturdays, but only occasionally was there a train service on a Sunday.

BRENT and KINGSBRIDGE.—Great Western.

Fares. 1 cl.	2 cl.	gov	Down.	mrn	mrn	aft	aft	aft	aft
			Brent ....dep.	9 23	1025	1 5	4 5	5 58	8 11
0 8	0 6	0 2½	Avonwick	9 30	1033	1 12	4 12	6 5	8 21
1 3	0 11	0 5	Gara Bridge	9 38	1050	1 20	4 20	6 13	8 32
1 11	1 4	0 9	Loddiswell	9 48	11 1	1 30	4 30	6 23	8 47
2 9	1 11	1 0¼	Kingsbridge ......arr.	10 0	1113	1 42	4 42	6 35	8 59

Fares. 1 cl.	2 cl.	gov	Up.	mrn	mrn	aft	aft	aft	
			Kingsbridge .....dep.	8 17	1150	2 33	4 55	6 45	....
0 10	0 7	0 3½	Loddiswell	8 28	12 1	2 44	5 7	6 56	....
1 8	1 2	0 7¼	Gara Bridge	8 37	1210	2 53	5 19	7 5	....
2 1	1 6	0 10	Avonwick	8 46	1219	3 2	5 30	7 14	....
2 9	1 11	1 0¼	Brent 24, 22.....arr.	8 54	1227	3 10	5 38	7 22	....

November 1894

BRENT and KINGSBRIDGE.—Great Western.

Miles	Down.	Week Days. mrn	mrn	aft	aft	aft	aft			
	Brent ....dep.	9 20	1030	1 10	4 5	6 8	8 35	....	....	....
2½	Avonwick	9 27	1037	1 18	4 12	6 15	8 42	....	....	....
5	Gara Bridge	9 35	1045	1 27	4 20	6 23	8 50	....	....	....
9	Loddiswell	9 43	1055	1 37	4 28	6 31	8 58	....	....	....
12½	Kingsbridge *.arr.	9 55	11 7	1 50	4 40	6 43	9 10	....	....	....

Miles	Up.	Week Days. mrn	mrn	mrn	aft	aft	aft		
	Kingsbridge ..dep.	8 0	9 15	1120	2 30	5 5	7 25	....	....
3½	Loddiswell	8 11	9 26	1131	2 41	5 17	7 36	....	....
7¼	Gara Bridge	8 19	9 35	1139	2 49	5 27	7 44	....	....
10	Avonwick	8 27	9 43	1147	2 57	5 36	7 52	....	....
12½	Brent 34, 32..arr.	8 35	9 51	1155	3 5	5 45	8 0	....	....

* Station for Salcombe, Torcross, and Slapton.

November 1904

BRENT and KINGSBRIDGE.—Great Western.

Miles	Down.	Week Days only. mrn	mrn		aft	a	aft	aft	aft	aft					
	Brent ....dep.	8 23	1025	....	1230	3 11	4 10	5 33	7 5	8 30	....	....	....	....	....
2½	Avonwick...............	8 30	1032	....	1237	3 18	4 17	5 41	7 12	8 37	....	....	....	....	....
5½	Gara Bridge............	8 38	1040	....	1245	3 26	4 27	5 52	7 25	8 45	....	....	....	....	....
9	Loddiswell.............	8 47	1049	....	1254	3 35	4 36	6 1	7 34	8 54	....	....	....	....	....
12½	Kingsbridge ‡ ....arr.	8 58	11 0	....	1 5	3 46	4 47	6 12	7 45	9 5	....	....	....	....	....

Miles	Up.	Week Days only. mrn	mrn	mrn	mrn		aft	aft	aft						
	Kingsbridge .....dep.	7 25	9 16	11 5	1140	....	2 35	4 5	7 0	....	....	....	....	....	....
3½	Loddiswell............	7 36	9 26	1116	1151	....	2 46	4 16	7 16	....	....	....	....	....	....
7	Gara Bridge...........	7 44	9 34	1124	1159	....	2 54	4 28	7 26	....	....	....	....	....	....
10	Avonwick..............	7 52	9 42	1132	12 7	....	3 2	4 37	7 34	....	....	....	....	....	....
12½	Brent 22, 27 .....arr.	8 0	9 50	1140	1215	....	3 10	4 46	7 42	....	....	....	....	....	....

NOTES.

a Runs on 19th instant, and daily on and after the 24th instant.

☞ A Service of Road Motor Cars runs between Kingsbridge Station and Salcombe.

‡ Station for Salcombe (6 miles), Thurlestone (4½ miles), Torcross (6½ miles), and Slapton (7½ miles).

July 1924

BRENT and KINGSBRIDGE.

Miles	Down.	Week Days only. mrn	mrn		aft	aft		aft		aft	
	Brent.........dep	825	1015	..	1215	3 6	..	6 0	..	8 30	..
2½	Avonwick..........	832	1022	..	1222	3 13	..	6 7	..	8 37	..
5½	Gara Bridge.......	840	1030	..	1230	3 21	..	6 15	..	8 45	..
9	Loddiswell.........	848	1038	..	1238	3 29	..	6 23	..	8 53	..
12½	Kingsbridge C arr.	859	1049	..	1249	3 40	..	6 34	..	9 4	..

Miles	Up.	Week Days only. mrn	mrn	mrn	Sats. only. aft	aft	aft	aft
	Kingsbridge..dep.	730	9 20	11 5	12 15	2 5	4 15	7 10
3½	Loddiswell........	740	9 30	1115	12 25	2 15	4 25	7 20
7	Gara Bridge.......	748	9 38	1123	12 33	2 23	4 33	7 28
10	Avonwick.........	756	9 46	1131	12 41	2 31	4 41	7 36
12½	Brent 26, 31..arr.	8 4	9 54	1139	12 49	2 39	4 49	7 44

C Station for Salcombe (6 miles), Thurlestone (4½ miles), Tolcross (6¼ miles), and Slapton (7½ miles).
A Service of Road Motor Cars runs between Kingsbridge and Salcombe.

August 1934

BRENT and KINGSBRIDGE.

Miles	Down	Week Days only. mrn		aft		aft	aft		aft	
	Brent,........ dep	8 25	..	1225	..	4 20	6 45	..	9 0	..
2½	Avonwick	8 32	..	1232	..	4 27	6 52	..	9 7	..
5½	Gara Bridge.......	8 40	..	1240	..	4 35	7 0	..	9 15	..
9	Loddiswell........	8 48	..	1248	..	4 43	7 8	..	9 23	..
12½	Kingsbridge C arr	8 59	..	1259	..	4 54	7 19	..	9 34	..

Miles	Up	Week Days only. mrn		mrn		aft	aft	aft		aft
	Kingsbridge...dep	7 30	..	11 0	..	2 0	4 15	5 30	..	8 0
3½	Loddiswell........	7 40	..	1110	..	2 10	4 25	5 40	..	8 10
7	Gara Bridge.......	7 48	..	1118	..	2 18	4 35	5 48	..	8 18
10	Avonwick	7 56	..	1126	..	2 26	4 43	5 56	..	8 26
12½	Brent 26, 31...arr	8 4	..	1134	..	2 34	4 51	6 4	..	8 34

C Station for Salcombe (6 miles), Thurlestone (4½ miles), Tolcross (6¼ miles), and Slapton (7½ miles).
A Service of Road Motor Cars runs between Kingsbridge and Salcombe.

BRENT and KINGSBRIDGE (for Salcombe)

January 1944

Week Days only

Miles		a.m	a.m S	p.m E	p.m S	p.m S	p.m S	p.m A	p.m	p.m S	p.m	p.m
—	**Brent** ... dep	8 20	9 48	1224	1234	1 20	2 10	4 15	5 20	6 5	7 0	9 20
2½	**Avonwick** ...	8 27	9 54	1230	1240	1 27	2 17	4 22	5 27	6 12	7 7	9 27
5½	**Gara Bridge** ...	8 35	10 2	1238	1248	1 35	2 27	4 32	5 35	6 22	7 15	9 35
9	**Loddiswell** ...	8 43	1010	1246	1256	1 43	2 35	4 41	5 43	6 30	7 23	9 43
12½	**Kingsbridge** ... arr	8 55	1025	1258	1 8	1 55	2 50	4 52	5 55	6 45	7 35	9 54
—	Salcombe ¶ ... arr	9 28	1058	1 28	1 58	2 28	3 28	5 28	6 28	7 28	8 28	11 3

Week Days only

Miles		a.m S	a.m E	a.m S	a.m W	a.m SB	a.m E	a.m S	non S	p.m	p.m	p.m	p.m S	p.m
	Salcombe ¶ ... dep	6 55	6 55	8 30	8 30	10 0	1030	1030	12 0	1 30	3 30	4 30	5 30	7 0
—	**Kingsbridge** ... dep	7 27	7 33	9 5	9 35	1055	11 5	1115	1230	2 10	4 15	5 15	6 5	7 45
3½	**Loddiswell** ...	7 37	7 43	9 15	9 45	..	1115	1125	1240	2 20	4 25	5 25	6 15	7 55
7	**Gara Bridge** ...	7 44	7 50	9 22	9 52	..	1122	1132	1248	2 27	4 33	5 33	6 22	8 3
10	**Avonwick** ...	7 53	7 59	9 30	10 0	..	1130	1140	1256	2 35	4 42	5 42	6 30	8 10
12½	**Brent** ... arr	8 1	8 7	9 40	1010	1130	1140	1150	1 5	2 45	4 50	5 51	6 40	8 19

A Through Carriages from London (Paddington) on Saturdays, depart 11 5 a.m. (Tables 61 and 81)
B Through Carriages to London (Paddington), arr. 4 15 p.m. (Tables 81 and 61)
E Except Saturdays
S Saturdays only
W Wednesdays only

¶ By Western National Omnibus (6 miles)

Road Services are also operated from Kingsbridge to Thurlestone and Hope

BRENT and KINGSBRIDGE (for Salcombe)

(Second class only except where otherwise shewn)

June 1950

WEEK DAYS ONLY

Miles		am	am S	am E	pm S	pm S	pm	pm G	pm E	pm S	pm S	pm S	pm E	pm S	pm E	pm S
—	**Brent** ... dep	8 20	9 55	1010	1234	1 20	2 10	3 40	4 0	4 38	5 35	6 10	6 45	7 18	9 15	9 20
2½	Avonwick ...	8 27	10 1	1017	1240	1 27	2 17	3 47	4 7	4 46	5 42	6 17	6 52	7 25	9 22	9 27
5½	Gara Bridge ...	8 35	10 9	1025	1248	1 35	2 25	3 55	4 15	4 54	5 50	6 27	7 0	7 33	9 30	9 35
9	Loddiswell ...	8 43	1017	1033	1256	1 43	2 33	4 3	4 23	5 2	5 58	6 36	7 8	7 41	9 38	9 43
12½	**Kingsbridge** ... arr	8 55	1030	1046	1 8	1 55	2 47	4 15	4 35	5 15	6 10	6 50	7 20	7 52	9 49	9 54
—	Salcombe ¶ ... arr	9 28	1058	1128	1 58	2 28	3 28	4 58	5 33	5 58	6 58	8 3	8 53	8 28	11 3	11 3

Miles		am	am S	am E	am H	am E	am S	am S	pm S	pm E	pm S	pm E	pm S	pm E	pm S
	Salcombe ¶ ... dep	6 55	8 27	8 27	10 0	1030	1030	1130	1 30	2 30	4 0	4 30	5 0	7 2	7 30
—	**Kingsbridge** ... dep	7 26	9 5	9 25	1055	11 0	1115	1230	2 10	3 0	4 35	5 15	5 30	7 40	7 57
3½	Loddiswell ...	7 36	9 15	9 35	..	11 8	1125	1240	2 20	3 10	4 45	5 25	5 40	7 50	8 7
7	Gara Bridge ...	7 43	9 22	9 42	..	1116	1132	1249	2 27	3 18	4 53	5 35	5 50	7 58	8 15
10	Avonwick ...	7 52	9 30	9 50	..	1124	1140	1257	2 35	3 26	5 0	5 43	5 58	8 6	8 23
12½	**Brent** ... arr	8 0	9 40	10 0	1130	1135	1150	1 5	2 45	3 35	5 10	5 51	6 6	8 15	8 31

E Except Saturdays
G Saturdays only. Through Carriages (First and Second class) London (Pad.) dep 11 0 am (Table 81)

H Saturdays only. Through Carriages (First and Second class) to London (Pad.) arr 4 18 pm (Table 81)

S Saturdays only
¶ By Western National Omnibus (Heavy luggage not conveyed)

Road Services are also operated from Kingsbridge to Thurlestone and Hope

BRENT and KINGSBRIDGE (for Salcombe)

June 1961

WEEK DAYS ONLY (Second class only)

MONDAYS TO FRIDAYS

Miles		am	am	pm	pm	pm	pm
—	**Brent** ... dep	7 20	9 45	1215	1 25	5 15	6 40
2½	Avonwick ...	7 26	9 51	1221	1 31	5 21	6 46
5½	Gara Bridge ...	7 33	9 58	1228	1 38	5 28	6 53
9	Loddiswell Halt ...	7 41	10 6	1236	1 46	5 36	7 1
12½	**Kingsbridge** ... arr	7 50	1015	1245	1 55	5 45	7 10
—	Salcombe ¶ ... arr	8 25	1058	1 28	2 28	6 33	8 3

SATURDAYS

	am	am	am	am	pm	pm	pm T	pm	pm	pm
Brent ... dep	6 52	8 20	9 48	1135	1 20	3 55	5 15	6 55	8 5	9 20
Avonwick ...	6 58	8 27	9 54	1141	1 26	4 1	5 22	7 1	8 11	9 26
Gara Bridge ...	7 5	8 35	10 1	1148	1 33	4 8	5 30	7 8	8 18	9 33
Loddiswell Halt ...	7 13	8 43	10 9	1156	1 41	4 16	5 38	7 16	8 26	9 41
Kingsbridge ... arr	7 22	8 54	1018	12 5	1 50	4 25	5 49	7 25	8 35	9 50
Salcombe ¶ ... arr	8 25	9 28	1058	1 28	2 28	4 58	6 33	8 3	9 58	11 3

MONDAYS TO FRIDAYS

Miles		am B	am	am	pm B	pm	pm A
	Salcombe ¶ ... dep	6 55	9 30	1130	1 30	5 0	6 0
—	**Kingsbridge** ... dep	8 0	1025	1250	2 5	5 53	7 20
3½	Loddiswell Halt ...	8 10	1035	1 0	2 15	6 3	7 30
7	Gara Bridge ...	8 16	1041	1 6	2 21	6 9	7 36
10	Avonwick ...	8 23	1048	1 13	2 28	6 16	7 43
12½	**Brent** ... arr	8 30	1055	1 20	2 35	6 23	7 50

SATURDAYS

	am	am T	am	am	pm	pm	pm A	pm	pm
Salcombe ¶ ... dep	6 55	8 27	9 30	1130	2 0	4 0	5 0	7 2	8 7
Kingsbridge ... dep	7 27	9 10	1025	1210	2 35	4 35	6 0	7 30	8 40
Loddiswell Halt ...	7 37	9 20	1035	1220	2 45	4 45	6 10	7 40	8 50
Gara Bridge ...	7 43	9 28	1041	1226	2 51	4 51	6 18	7 46	8 56
Avonwick ...	7 50	9 36	1048	1233	2 58	4 58	6 26	7 53	9 3
Brent ... arr	7 57	9 44	1055	1240	3 5	5 5	6 34	8 0	9 10

A To Newton Abbot (Table 81)
B To Totnes (Table 81)

T Through carriages from or to Paddington (Table 81). First and Second class

¶ By Western National Omnibus (Heavy luggage not conveyed)

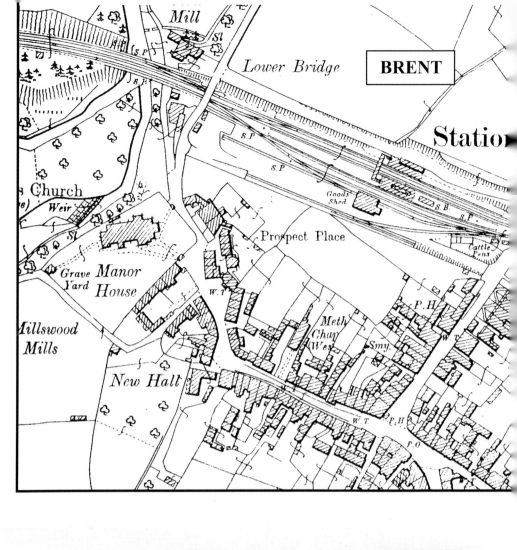

BRENT

Mill

Lower Bridge

Station

Church

Weir

Grave Yard

Manor House

Millswood Mills

New Hall

Prospect Place

Goods Shed

S.B.

Cattle Pens

P.H.

Meth Chap (Wes

Smy.

W.T.

P.H.

P.O.

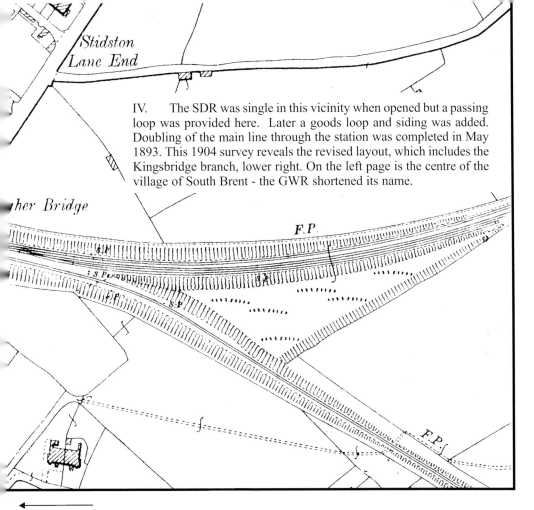

Stidston
Lane End

IV.   The SDR was single in this vicinity when opened but a passing loop was provided here. Later a goods loop and siding was added. Doubling of the main line through the station was completed in May 1893. This 1904 survey reveals the revised layout, which includes the Kingsbridge branch, lower right. On the left page is the centre of the village of South Brent - the GWR shortened its name.

her Bridge

F.P.

1.   Our first group of photographs are undated, but appear to be from the early years of the 20th century, some of them probably having been produced as postcards. This eastward view features an up train, while the branch coaches stand with doors open. (Lens of Sutton)

2.   All the buildings date from 1893, including the 66-lever signal box. The up train appears to be hauled by no. 172, a 4-4-2 built in 1905 and named *Quicksilver* and renamed *The Abbot* in 1907. (Lens of Sutton)

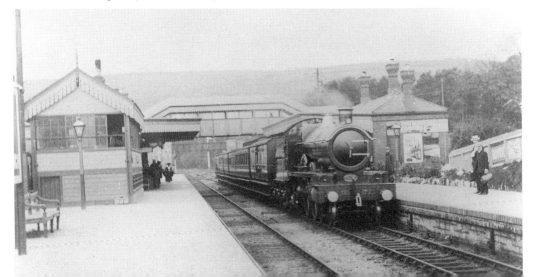

3.   A substantial train of cattle wagons stands in the long siding while animals are gathered for transit. The branch train appears to be composed of four-wheelers and there is little spare space in the yard. (Lens of Sutton)

4.   Branch services were worked mainly by 2-6-2Ts. This is no. 3104; one other member of the 3100 class was recorded on the route regularly, it being no. 3101. They were built as part of the 3150 class, introduced in 1907. (Lens of Sutton)

5.   No. 3185 was recorded taking water at the up platform. Four BR 2-6-2Ts were recorded in the line's final years: 82006, 82009, 82029 and 82033. All locomotives were based at Newton Abbot. (Lens of Sutton)

6.   Long shadows help to emphasise the rough surface of the island platform, which made movement of heavily laden barrows difficult. An up train is arriving and is about to receive the contents of one. (Lens of Sutton)

→

7.   Some help was available for the handling of heavy items in the goods shed. Featured is the hand operated crane which was rated at 30cwt. (1½ tons). No. 3104 was photographed in about 1906. It was later renumbered 4404 and it lasted until 1952. (R.S.Carpenter coll.)

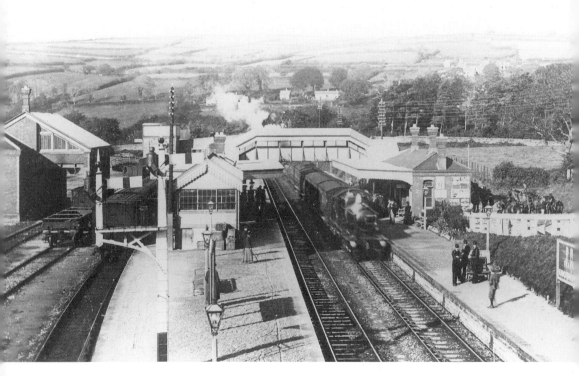

→

8.   This wide angle view is included to show most of the long siding on the left and the approach road on the right. The southern flank of Dartmoor is in the background. (Lens of Sutton)

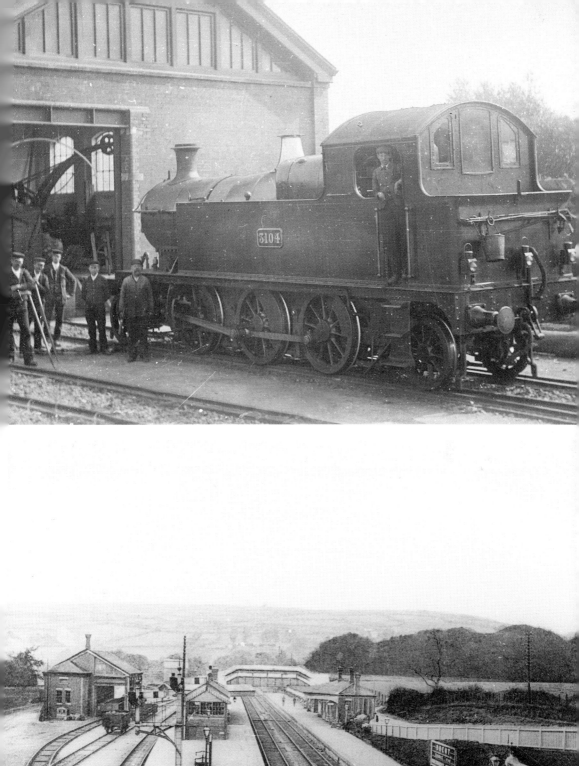

9.   Shown in the working timetables for many years were two such "Mixed Trains", that is comprising both goods and passenger vehicles. Later regulations required the freight to be at the back, unless vacuum braked. (Lens of Sutton)

10.   An up express was recorded on th gradient down into the station, as it passed unde the road to Aish. We have the opportunity o seeing the position of the water column and tank (Lens of Sutton)

11.   Steam railmotors were introduced by the GWR in 1903 and no. 45 was finished in 1905. It usually operated on the Plymouth suburban service, but it ran one return trip between Saltash and Kingsbridge at one period. Withdrawal was in 1927. (W.R.Gray/K.A.Williams coll.)

←

12.　A photograph from 1st May 1925 shows the goods yard to be particularly congested. The locomotive is no. 4474, an LNER class A3 4-6-2 on an exchange trial. It was named *Victor Wild*. (Lens of Sutton)

←

13.　We now jump to 18th August 1953 and can enjoy the sight of 4-6-0 no. 6949 *Haberfield Hall*. This locomotive had been converted to oil burning for a short period, when it was numbered 3955. Note that Salcombe is mentioned on the running-in board. (K.A.Williams coll.)

14.　This westward view includes the up refuge loop which had been just a siding until 1937 and was to revert to that status again in 1972. The corresponding bridge at the other end of the station had been a bowstring structure until 1952. (K.A.Williams)

15.　The replacement bridge is evident as 2-6-2T no. 4562 runs towards the branch train on 17th April 1958. The cattle pens, seen earlier in picture no. 3, were no longer whitened and were seldom used. (R.S.Carpenter)

16.　The up side building was not of the flamboyant style employed by other companies. Featured here is the east elevation and also included is the bridge shown in picture 14. (HMRS)

17.　Caught simmering gently on 8th September 1958 is 2-6-2T no. 5533 after arrival from Kingsbridge. Some of the passengers are waiting for a train to Plymouth. The staff dropped from 22 to 17 during the 1950s. (R.N.Joanes/K.A.Williams coll.)

18.   No. 4561 was photographed on 3rd August 1959, whilst running round the branch train. It is about to run forward onto the coaches. The locomotive was saved for a new life on the West Somerset Railway. (M.Dart)

19.   The residence of the station master is in the background. From this elevated position, his empire could be kept under observation. Note the spacious rodding tunnels to the signal box machine room. The box closed on 17th December 1973. (K.A.Williams coll.)

20.   The crew of 2-6-2T no. 5558 stretch out in the sunshine in June 1960, while the down Ocean Liner Express passes on its way to Plymouth. The coach on the right has the corner positioned doors of the saloons used on that service. (H.Cowan/M.Dart)

21.   An eastward view of the up side includes the entrance for local residents. There were only 1360 of them in 1901 and 1803 in 1961. The building no longer exists, but the goods shed became a dental surgery and the yard an industrial estate. The surgery was named "Primrose Junction", as the route was known as the "Primrose Line". (K.A.Williams)

22.   The GWR was generally considerate to its passengers by usually providing at least a roof to the footbridge. Full protection was provided here, as at many other junctions. (K.A.Williams)

23.   An unusual event was recorded on the first Monday of regular local diesel service. The final steam hauled branch coach was brought back from Kingsbridge ignominiously in the goods train. This was Spring 1961. (K.A.Williams coll.)

24.   Steam on the branch continued for freigh
traffic and also for through coaches to and from
London on Summer Saturdays. Diesels were

making inroads into the locomotive fleet on the main line in 1961. This example appears to be D847. (K.A.Williams coll.)

25.   Single Gloucester railcar no. W55000 was working the branch on 5th July 1962. It was later preserved and can usually be found at Buckfastleigh. Five passengers joined the train here and six more en route. It was the 9.45am departure. No freight is evident - official withdrawal was on 6th April 1964. (B.Jennings)

26.   The final steam train on the branch departed at 6.55pm on 10th September 1963 and was hauled by 2-6-2T no. 4555, now preserved on the Paignton & Dartmouth Railway. Four coaches of "The Cornishman" were hired privately for 85 people to "Ride & Dine". (B.Gibson)

EAST OF BRENT

27.   A "Saint" class 4-6-0 approaches the station with a down train in about 1910, the track plan being that shown on map IV. The signal arms carrying an S allowed shunting movements, while the ringed one was for goods trains leaving the down refuge siding. (K.A.Williams coll.)

**Other views of this station
are included in our
Newton Abbot to Plymouth album.**

28.   The 7.30pm from Kingsbridge arrives behind no. 4561 on 8th June 1961 and is passing over the connection which had been added for wartime traffic on 17th August 1943. The refuge siding had been extended to form a long loop in April 1933. (P.W.Gray)

29.   An early postcard featured a 517 class 0-4-2T about to pass under the main road (A38 from 1919) with a train from Kingsbridge. The line snakes away in the distance. (Lens of Sutton coll.)

30.   The preserved "Prairie", no. 4561, features in this and the next two pictures, although they were taken on different days. This is the 10.10am from Brent passing under the next bridge on the branch on 27th May 1961, the line turning south at this point. The bridge carried a lane known as Plymouth Old Road. (P.W.Gray)

31.   We can now enjoy the sight of the 9.25am from Kingsbridge climbing away from Avonwick on 19th April 1960. Both coaches have 1st class accommodation and both vans are four-wheelers, the leading one being of Eastern Region origin. (P.W.Gray)

32.   The 5.40pm from Kingsbridge often conveyed vans carrying crabs and lobsters destined for London and also for Southampton for the luxury liners. The locomotive is accelerating from its Avonwick stop on 8th June 1961. (P.W.Gray)

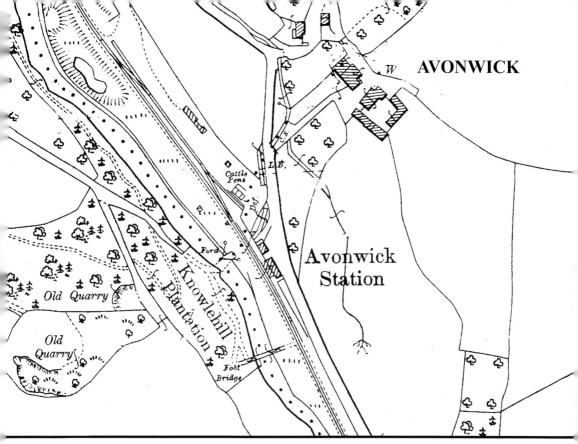

AVONWICK

V.   The 1904 survey includes the cattle pens which are not visible in the photographs. The name Avonwick came into use in about 1878; the parish is North Huish and its population rose from 317 in 1901 to 355 in 1961.

33.   An up train is in the distance as a dutiful station master observes that all is in order. The staff level seldom exceeded one. (Lens of Sutton)

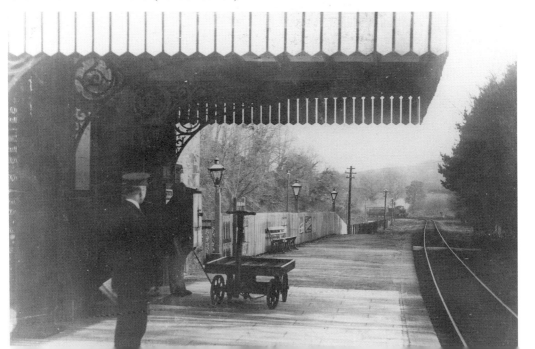

34.   Steam from the injector largely obscures the guard as the crew of the 0-4-2T enjoy the status of being photographed. Gentlemen could marvel at the fine quoins on the doorway on the right. (Lens of Sutton)

35.   It seems that one barrow was sufficient for the milk churns and parcels being presented. This 1921 view includes a van and a wagon, rare items in later photographs. (Lens of Sutton)

Avonwick	1903	1913	1923	1933
Passenger tickets issued	6896	7198	5734	3873
Season tickets issued	*	*	39	10
Parcels forwarded	3232	4406	4956	1865
General goods forwarded (tons)	170	201	35	28
General goods received (tons)	333	764	376	185
Trucks of livestock handled	14	25	16	5

(* not available.)

36.   We now have three photographs from the early 1950s. All three intermediate stations were provided with camp coaches in 1934; they were termed camping coaches later. The ground frame and crossover were removed in April 1955. (J.H.Moss/R.S.Carpenter)

37. No. 4582 departs south and briefly disturbs the peace at this tranquil spot. Note that a clean patch on the end of the coach indicates that the set was dedicated to the branch. (J.Scott-Morgan coll./R.S.Carpenter)

38. It seems that there was good provision made for heating the building and that the telegraph and/or telephone system had grown beyond that seen in picture 29. (J.H.Moss/R.S.Carpenter)

39. Staffing ceased on 11th June 1956, parcels and goods facilities being withdrawn at that time. No. 5558 was recorded with one van and two coaches in June 1959. (H.Cowan/M.Dart)

40.	No. 4561 was working the 10.10am from Brent when recorded running alongside the lane to Diptford on 1st August 1960. This is now a WSR star performing locomotive. (P.W.Gray)

41.	No. 5525 would be scrapped not long after being photographed with the 2.10pm from Kingsbridge on 26th August 1961. A stream runs between the fences on the right and passes under the platform. (S.P.Derek)

42.	The goods shed had more substantial quoins than the main building, but by the 1960s its only purpose was to support a timetable poster and a redundant lamp bracket. (Lens of Sutton)

43.   Alterations during the final decade included modernising the canopy valencing and removal of the massive ivy growth from the goods shed. The seat castings still declared defiantly "GWR". (Lens of Sutton)

44.   The final through train from Paddington was hauled by a D6300 class diesel on 31st August 1963. It called at 5.38pm on a dismal Saturday. (B.Gibson)

45.   The buildings were saved from demolition to become joined to form a dwelling. The doorway for loading goods to and from road vehicles has been infilled by the window on the right of this view from the 1980s. (E.D.Reynolds)

SOUTH OF AVONWICK

46.   Three landscape studies emphasise the charm of the environs of the small village of Diptford. No. 4561 runs close to the Avon with the 4.55pm from Brent on 8th June 1961. (P.W.Gray)

47.   The same locomotive appears in all three views. It is passing Broadley Farm on 5th March 1960, hauling the 2.30pm from Brent. The coach does not appear to contain any passengers. (P.W.Gray)

48.   Numerous travellers are enjoying the scenery on 1st August 1960, as the 11.0am from Kingsbridge ambles northward, leaving exhaust to delight any photographer. (P.W.Gray)

GARA BRIDGE

Gara Bridge	1903	1913	1923	1933	1943	1953	1958
Passenger tickets issued	4782	5225	5787	3672	4370	2715	2950
Season tickets issued	*	*	11	60	47	58	142
Parcels forwarded	2920	3403	3143	1399	312	256	377
General goods forwarded (tons)	624	786	325	105	206	*	*
General goods received (tons)	871	1145	604	156	799	*	*
Trucks of livestock handled	23	30	23	5	*	*	*

(* not available.)

VI.   The 1904 survey confirms that there was little habitation near the station. The dots of the parish boundary are in the centre of the River Avon. The station is in Diptford parish, which housed 502 souls in 1901, but only 318 by 1961.

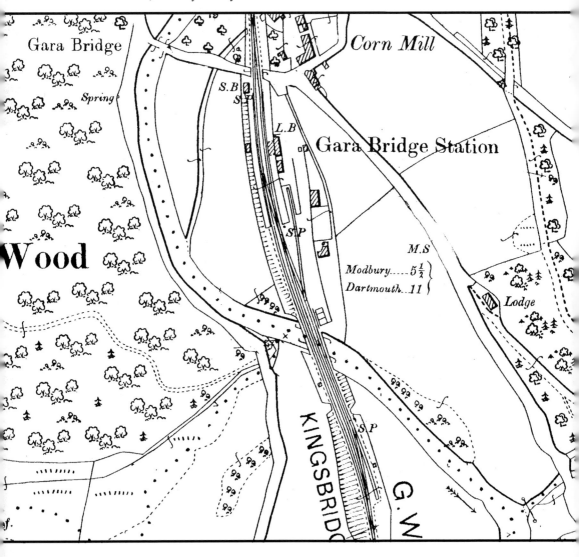

49.	A postcard view looks across the river and features the house provided for the station master, on the right. Three men were usually employed here. (Lens of Sutton)

50.	The architectural details were similar to those used at the neighbouring stations. A notable difference is that the goods shed had roof lights. The photograph is from 1921. (Lens of Sutton)

51. The detailed ornamentation applied to utilitarian objects is worthy of study. The lantern flue was surmounted by a thistle and the roof corners decorated with perforated oak leaves. The entire case was suspended in an iron framework. The front glass carries the station name. (LGRP/NRM)

52. The station master poses with two staff members (plus daughter?) in the two-tone paint era. Baskets for local produce are near the goods shed. (Lens of Sutton)

53.   This postcard was intended to convey the charm of the Avon Valley, rather than the detail of rolling stock. However, it does include a clerestory coach on an up train, suggesting an early date. (Cookworthy Museum)

54.   The words CAMP COACH date the photograph as likely to be between 1934 and 39. They were provided with paraffin for lighting, cooking and heating. The pole in the foreground was probably carrying an aerial wire for a wireless set. (D.J.Hyde/K.A.Williams coll.)

55. Nature was encroaching on the down platform by the 1950s, but signal sighting had not become a problem due to low speeds. The arm on the left was for the goods loop. (Lens of Sutton)

56. As there was no footbridge, the crossing for passengers was placed within sight of the signalman. The gates swung across the B3207, a quiet road between Modbury and Halwell. (J.H.Moss/R.S.Carpenter)

57.   Happy holidaymakers wait by a train bound for Kingsbridge in about 1958. Four different
Pannier Tanks were known to have worked the branch, nos. 2062, 3796, 9633 and 9678.
(K.A.Williams coll.)

58.   We make no apology for including another panorama, as this was one of the most delightfully situated stations of GWR origin. The attractive road bridge over the Avon can also be spotted. (K.A.Williams coll.)

59.   Trains passed here regularly in the Summer, ten coaches being accommodated easily. However, on occasions some were formed of fourteen. No. 5533 was recorded in August 1959. (H.Cowan/M.Dart)

60.   August 1960 and the up platform is becoming overwhelmed by cupressus trees. Like all good things, they are best in moderation. (R.E.Toop)

61.   No. 4561 has just passed over the river on its way to Kingsbridge with the 2.30pm from Brent on 8th June 1961. A destination board is between the two first class compartments. (P.W.Gray)

62.   Passing on 21st June 1961 is no. 5564 with an up freight and no. W55017, still with gleaming paintwork and its "cats whiskers". A fresh-water can stands on the platform, as there was no mains supply here. (J.H.Meredith)

63.   Seen on the same day is coach no. W9902W. By that time cooking was by Calo[r] Gas, but those needing a bath had to wait for a[n] invitation to the home of a friendly railyman[?]. Note that the doors have been sealed this side[.] (J.H.Meredith)

64.   Peace and tranquility was assured for the campers who would have an unusual holiday under the loading gauge. The signalman would order groceries to be delivered by the next train. The charge was £12 per week, but six adult tickets had to be purchased. (Lens of Sutton)

65.   The enthusiastic staff laid out gardens, the edging of which was made from granite setts recovered from the long closed Plymouth tram tracks. The last let ended on 14th October 1962, during which year there was only one coach present. (K.A.Williams coll.)

66.   The humorous photographer created the PING COACH, but Pong Coach would be more apt after many lets, it seems. The station staff had to undertake the cleaning and provide fresh bed linen every Saturday. (K.A.Williams coll.)

67.   The signal box was fitted with a 24-lever frame and is seen after repainting by BR. Dark red glass was fitted to the lamp on the right, to warn motorists of the presence of the level crossing. (K.A.Williams)

68.   The existence of a gate wheel speeded proceedings and helped to maintain good timekeeping. The vertical rack was part of the gate lock mechanism. (P.W.Gray)

69.   Two views from the final Winter feature the trackwork fully, as no stock was present. Both include the derelict cattle pens. (K.A.Williams)

70.	Both down starting signals are evident, but the one on the left was seldom used. The permanent way was well maintained to the end. (K.A.Williams)

71.	A few days after closure, a stores train was run to collect all equipment, furniture and indoor materials from the stations. The train is in deep shadow for the sombre occasion. The buildings became a dwelling. (B.Gibson)

SOUTH OF GARA BRIDGE

72.   Bound for Brent on Easter Monday 1960
is no. 4561. The small signal on the bracket is
for Gara Bridge goods loop. (M.J.Esau)

73.   Topsham Ground Frame controlled a little used crossing more than a mile from Gara Bridge. The lamp had two red glasses and is being inspected in 1964. (B.Gibson)

74.   The track approaching Loddiswell won the Prize Length Award in 1958, this justifying a photograph. The village is in the background, across the valley. (K.A.Williams coll.)

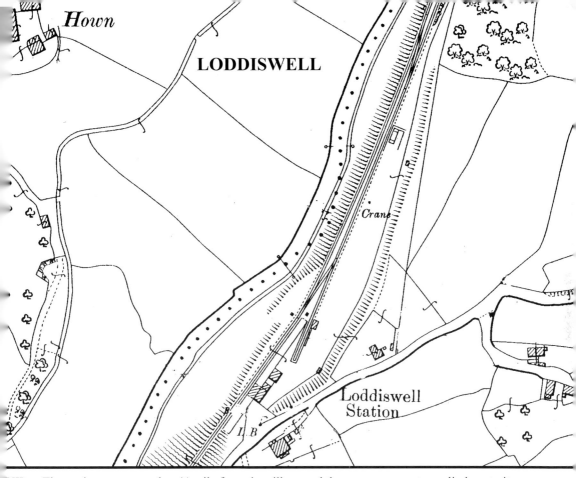

VII.   The station was more than ½ mile from the village and there was a very steep climb up to its main street. This 1905 edition shows that there were a few dwellings nearby. The population of the parish was 650 in 1901, but only 637 in 1961.

75.   The lane on the east side of the valley climbed on a severe gradient behind the station to the small community of Woodleigh. The line was almost on the floor of the valley and there were two mills nearby. (Lens of Sutton coll.)

76.   A 1921 view includes a down freight train near the ground frame hut and also a post with lamp frame, but no lantern. The name has a silent "i" - *Lodswell*, when used by locals. There was a staff of two here between the wars.
(Lens of Sutton)

77.   Seen in the early 1950s, the gardens were well tended and there were hanging flowe[r] baskets as well. The wooden bodied cars of tha[t] era were termed "station wagons", apt in this case[.]
(J.H.Moss/R.S.Carpenter)

Loddiswell	1903	1913	1923	1933
Passenger tickets issued	7941	8902	8327	5220
Season tickets issued	*	*	31	122
Parcels forwarded	2069	2918	2720	1457
General goods forwarded (tons)	308	370	192	59
General goods received (tons)	1146	945	583	421
Trucks of livestock handled	30	31	7	22

(* not available.)

78.   Moving down the platform, we note the hut for the permanent way trolley and that the one for the ground frame is in pieces on the ground, leaving the two levers exposed. A busy goods yard is probably an illusion - it is likely that the vans are being stored. (J.H.Moss/R.S.Carpenter)

79.   The strategic placing of the house for the station master is very evident in this photograph from June 1959. Less clear is that he has the photographer under observation, and so has the driver of no. 5533. (H.Cowan/M.Dart)

———————▶

80.   This fine panorama is from 16th April 1960 and includes no. 4561 with the 11.0am from Kingsbridge. The yard had been busy during World War II with supplies for the US Army and the Royal Navy, and subsequently with telegraph poles and water pipes for improved local services. (P.W.Gray)

———————▶

81.   There was one camping coach in 1952-57 and two in 1958-61. In the background are the cattle pens. They may have been used in 1940 when the 25th Animal Transport Company of the Indian Army arrived for a stay in Woodleigh Monastery. Wheat from Manitoba arrived here after the war for milling locally. (K.A.Williams coll.)

82.   We can enjoy a final look at the fine stonework and seat castings as a Gloucester railcar calls in 1962. Staffing ceased on 4th September 1961 resulting in "Halt" status, but this did not appear on the signs. (Lens of Sutton)

83.   As at Avonwick, the two historic structures were joined to form a spacious dwelling. At least they survive. These private properties must not be visited. (E.D.Reynolds)

84.   On the last day of operation, the usual railcar was supplemented by a 2-car DMU. They were recorded on the embankment, where the line leaves the Avon Valley. The B3196 runs under the bridge. (B.Gibson)

85. The north end of Sorley Tunnel was recorded as work began in 1891, the first sod having been cut in January of that year. Springs were encountered during the blasting and digging, but drainage was no problem. (K.A.Williams coll.)

86. The north portal of the 625yd Sorley Tunnel was a fine and under appreciated work of the masons' skill. The summit was mid-way through it and down goods trains were required to stop beyond the tunnel to have the wagon brakes pinned down for the descent to the terminus. (K.A.Williams coll.)

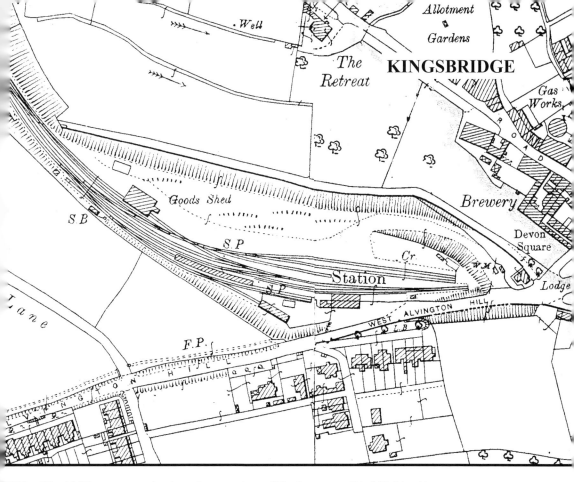

VIII.   The 1905 survey emphasises the curvature of the layout on this hillside site.

87.   It seems that the station is almost ready for opening, even the nameboard is in place. No longer will travel to Plymouth be a choice between the twice weekly boat or a rough ride to Kingsbridge Road station, later named Wrangaton. (Cookworthy Museum)

Kingsbridge	1903	1913	1923	1933	1943	1953	1958
Passenger tickets issued	30358	33905	32069	18656	34397	14869	14163
Season tickets issued	*	*	22	95	29	246	58
Parcels forwarded	32213	56346	55141	106371	17631	26752	15692
General goods forwarded (tons)	2936	2650	4627	2233	10832	4617	2748
General goods received (tons)	5642	6718	11035	10322	28908	20866	9929
Trucks of livestock handled	309	459	382	222	*	*	*

(* not available.)

88.   This is the oldest operational view known and is of a mixed train, the rear two vehicles being a cattle wagon and a brake van. The track in the foreground was part of the proposed route to Salcombe, but was removed later. (Cookworthy Museum)

89.   A class 517 0-4-2T has just arrived and passengers emerge through the gate and pass the coach carrying the words SALCOMBE TO KINGSBRIDGE. It will presumably carry folk in the other direction as well. Bystanders look for friends arriving. (Lens of Sutton)

90.   A similar postcard view with the same class of locomotive is included as it features the Dartmouth coach, this requiring three horses. There is evidence that the usual unwelcome aroma is arising from the road. (Lens of Sutton)

91.   The GWR Magazine of 1907 stated "Rabbits are usually plentiful in the West of England, but this year they have been exceptionally so. Kingsbridge is a busy centre for rabbit traffic, and trappers, farmers, and dealers bring thither large quantities. The rabbits are packed in hampers, which hold from 20 to 24 brace and weigh about 1cwt. In the illustration a consignment of about 1 ton is seen ready for despatch". (GWR)

92.   The bogie van for rabbit traffic carried this dedicated roofboard. Less went to London - maybe Londoners could afford more agreeable food. (K.A.Williams coll.)

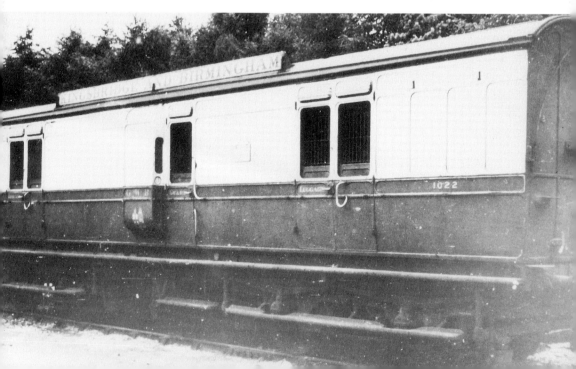

Gt Western Ry.	Gt. Western Ry
Loddiswell	Loddiswell

KINGSBRIDGE
THIRD CLASS
6d   Fare   6d
Issued subject to the conditions & regulations set
out in the Companys Time Tables Bills & Notices
Kingsbridge   Kingsbridge

2106 · 2106

Gt Western Ry	Gt. Western Ry.
Gara Bridge	Gara Bridge

B R E N T
5d, PARLY,(3rd Cls.) 5d,
Issued subject to the conditions & regu-
lations set out in the Company's Time
Tables Books and Bills.   (J.C.)
BRENT   BRENT

APL.30 95 · 539

93.   Apart from recording an animated scene, this panorama includes the partially open area of
the toilets and also their water tanks. This was altered during major changes in 1916.
(Lens of Sutton)

———————→

94.	The major improvement in 1916 was the provision of this bay platform. The other one was lengthened at the same time and the loop was extended greatly. Staff levels increased from 10 in 1913 to 16 in 1923 and 25 in 1934. (Lens of Sutton)

95.	The GWR was a pioneer with "Road Motors", starting in 1903. The first service from Kingsbridge was to Salcombe, commencing on 21st July 1909. Modbury followed on 14th October, Dartmouth on 30th June 1919 and Plymouth on 25th March 1921. Others followed and all became part of the GWR sponsored Western National in 1929. Seen near the buffers in 1923 is AEC no. 228. (K.A.Williams coll.)

———————→

96.	The cattle pens were originally between the engine shed and the platform, but after 1916 they were located on the north side of the site. In later years, the London coaches often stood in this siding from Sunday to Friday. No. 4582 was photographed in about 1947. (R.S.Carpenter)

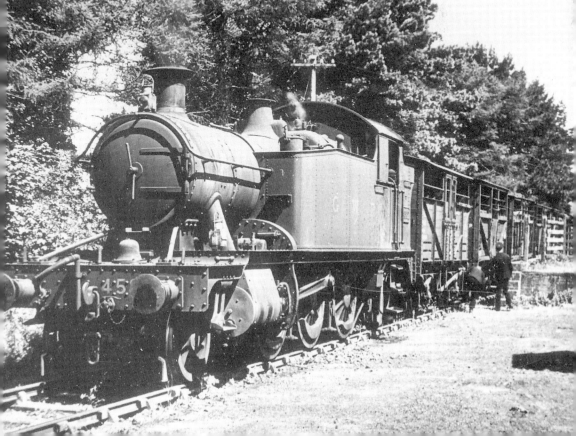

97.   This 1950 panorama should be compared with picture 93. Inexplicably, the new roof was to
a different pitch. The huts on the right housed locomotive stores, crew rest room and signing-on
office. (K.A.Williams coll.)

IX.   Diagram from the 1950s.

1.	Goods Shed	6.	Store
2.	Cattle Pens	7.	Station
3.	Motor Garage	8.	Engine Shed
4.	Crane	9.	Water tank
5.	Carriage shed	10.	Signal box

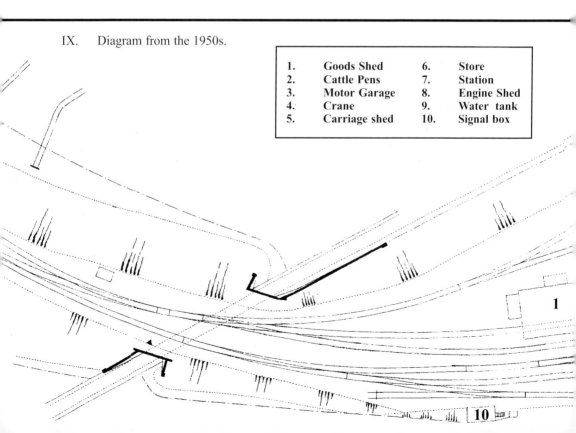

8. The goods shed had a large office and two sheltered loading bays. It contained the usual hand operated crane for large items and was recorded in 1958. (K.A.Williams)

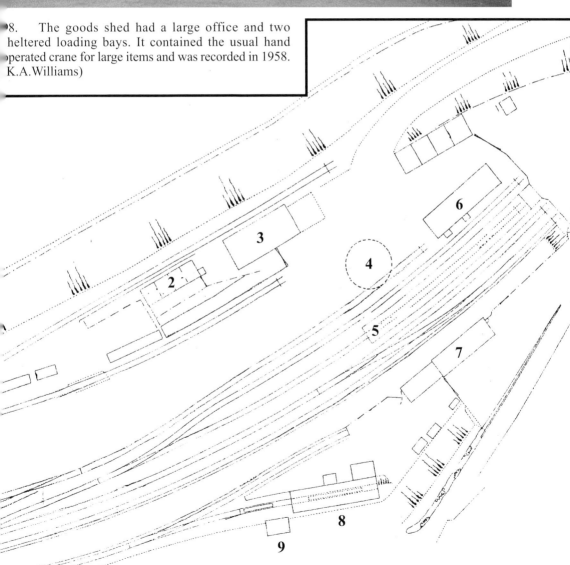

99.   Also seen in 1958 is the north elevation of the main building. From left to right: station master, booking office, waiting room, toilets and parcels office. (K.A.Williams)

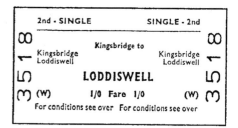

100.   Looking up, we can appreciate that the canopy extension had cantilevered steel joists instead of cast iron brackets. Illumination was by Suggs shadow-free globe gas lights, with chain operated cocks and bypass flames. (K.A.Williams)

101.   Mailbags are the only sign of potential revenue in this picture from 16th August 1958. Note the revised position of the engine release points in comparison with that seen in picture 88. (E.Wilmshurst)

102. We have seen no. 5558 before, but not the line to the bay platform or the west elevation of the goods shed and its security door. (R.C.Riley)

103.   No. 5533 is standing close to the buffer stops while running round its coaches on 17th April 1958. Another GWR branch to end on an embankment for a projected extension southwards was the one to Helston. (R.S.Carpenter)

104.   We now have two photographs from 1958 The signal box had a 30-lever frame and changed little over the years. However, the steps had always been painted dark brown by the GWR (K.A.Williams)

105.   The revised position of the buffers is featured here, along with a Western National Bristol working the routes established by the GWR more than 30 years earlier. Despite this time interval, some busmen still retained their NUR membership. (K.A.Williams)

106. No. 5533 waits to depart in June 1959, while we look at the continuation of the carriage shed from the previous picture. London trains often had to be divided into three for storage. (H.Cowan/M.Dart)

107. Two shots from 1961 show almost the fu extent of the trackwork. A diesel rests in the ba between freight workings. The yard ha despatched up to 1000 tons of cider apple annually in the 1930s. (K.A.Williams)

108. A northward panorama includes the entire "throat". The curvature helped the shunter signal to the driver, except on the far siding. (K.A.Williams coll.)

109.   The engine shed could house only one locomotive and it closed in September 1961, although the pit was sometimes used subsequently. Below the coal stage is an awkwardly sited catch point. (Lens of Sutton)

110.   This is the 10.55 (Saturdays only) throug train leaving for Paddington on 24th June 196 with no. 5573 in charge. Another catch point i evident. (S.P.Derek)

111.   Sugar beet traffic began in 1941 and several wagon loads were despatched each day in subsequent seasons. A diesel proceeds towards loaded wagons in the bay in this 1961 view from the signal box steps. In the background is the 6-ton yard crane and Silcock's cattle feed store, which was assembled from concrete components in about 1950. (K.A.Williams)

112.   No. 5573 is starting the run round process on 24th June 1961, having arrived with the 5.35pm from Brent. It will return at 6.15 with empty stock. Most trains were diesel powered by this time. (S.P.Derek)

113.   As elsewhere on the branch, the gardens were a joy to behold. Passengers waiting for a delayed train could find plenty for their pleasure. The gardens won 1st prize in 1960 and 2nd in the subsequent three years. (Lens of Sutton)

114.   Freight trains were much shorter in 1961 than previously due to inroads made by road transport. No. D6332 waits to depart with two vans and a "Toad". The last steam hauled freight ran on 11th July 1962. (Lens of Sutton)

115.   The starting signals retained tapered wooden posts to the end. This picture is included to show the walkway and its lamp provided for the signalman to use when handling the single line token. (Lens of Sutton)

116.   Two views from 5th July 1962 reveal tha the station was kept in good order to the end Although electricity has arrived, the platforms were still gas lit. (B.Jennings)

117.   The nearest lamp had been dismantled as long trains no longer ran at night, but the fine gardens lasted until closure. The population of the town remained at about 3000 throughout the life of the line. (B.Jennings)

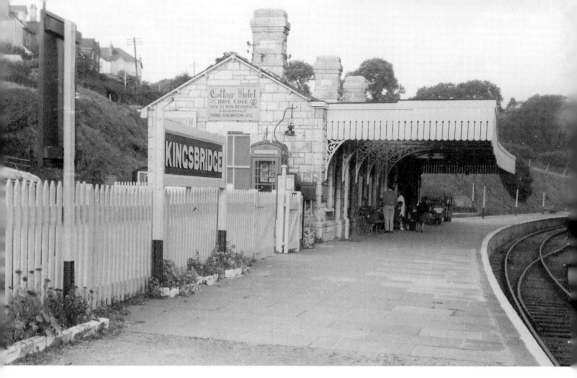

118.   A railcar smokes in the loop, only months before closure. It may be standing there awaiting the arrival of a freight train, such services lasting to the end. (Lens of Sutton)

119.   This shed only appears in the left background of picture 105 and is shown fully here after line closure. It was the GWR's road motor garage for buses and lorries, also being used for fodder in its early days. (K.A.Williams)

120.   To end on a happier note, we include one of the GWR's two boats used on their service to Salcombe, which operated in 1927-29. A railway booking office was maintained at Salcombe as late as 1961. The *Kenwith Castle* is being moored upon arrival at Kingsbridge. (K.A.Williams coll.)

3rd–SINGLE	SINGLE–3rd
Kingsbridge to	
Kingsbridge	Kingsbridge
Paddington	Paddington
PADDINGTON	
viaTaunton	
(W) 17/3 FARE 17/3 (W)	
ForConditions see over	ForConditions see over

MP Middleton Press

Easebourne Lane, Midhurst, W Sussex. GU29 9AZ Tel: 01730 813169 Fax: 01730 812601
*If books are not available from your local transport stockist, order direct with cheque,
Visa or Mastercard, post free UK.*

BRANCH LINES
Branch Line to Allhallows
Branch Line to Alton
Branch Lines around Ascot
Branch Line to Ashburton
Branch Lines around Bodmin
Branch Line to Bude
Branch Lines around Canterbury
Branch Lines around Chard & Yeovil
Branch Line to Cheddar
Branch Lines around Cromer
Branch Lines to East Grinstead
Branch Lines of East London
Branch Lines to Effingham Junction
Branch Lines around Exmouth
Branch Lines to Falmouth, Helston & St. Ives
Branch Line to Fairford
Branch Lines around Gosport
Branch Line to Hayling
Branch Lines to Henley, Windsor & Marlow
Branch Line to Hawkhurst
Branch Lines around Huntingdon
Branch Line to Ilfracombe
Branch Line to Kingsbridge
Branch Line to Kingswear
Branch Line to Lambourn
Branch Lines to Launceston & Princetown
Branch Line to Looe
Branch Line to Lyme Regis
Branch Lines around Midhurst
Branch Line to Minehead
Branch Line to Moretonhampstead
Branch Lines to Newport
Branch Lines to Newquay
Branch Lines around North Woolwich
Branch Line to Padstow
Branch Lines around Plymouth
Branch Lines to Seaton and Sidmouth
Branch Lines around Sheerness
Branch Line to Shrewsbury
Branch Line to Swanage *updated*
Branch Line to Tenterden
Branch Lines around Tiverton
Branch Lines to Torrington
Branch Line to Upwell
Branch Lines of West London
Branch Lines around Weymouth
Branch Lines around Wimborne
Branch Lines around Wisbech

NARROW GAUGE
Branch Line to Lynton
Branch Lines around Portmadoc 1923-46
Branch Lines around Porthmadog 1954-94
Branch Line to Southwold
Douglas to Port Erin
Douglas to Peel
Kent Narrow Gauge
Northern France Narrow Gauge
Romneyrail
Southern France Narrow Gauge
Sussex Narrow Gauge
Two-Foot Gauge Survivors
Vivarais Narrow Gauge

SOUTH COAST RAILWAYS
Ashford to Dover
Bournemouth to Weymouth
Brighton to Worthing
Eastbourne to Hastings
Hastings to Ashford
Portsmouth to Southampton
Ryde to Ventnor
Southampton to Bournemouth

SOUTHERN MAIN LINES
Basingstoke to Salisbury
Bromley South to Rochester
Crawley to Littlehampton
Dartford to Sittingbourne
East Croydon to Three Bridges
Epsom to Horsham
Exeter to Barnstaple
Exeter to Tavistock
Faversham to Dover
London Bridge to East Croydon
Orpington to Tonbridge
Tonbridge to Hastings
Salisbury to Yeovil
Sittingbourne to Ramsgate
Swanley to Ashford
Tavistock to Plymouth
Three Bridges to Brighton
Victoria to Bromley South
Victoria to East Croydon
Waterloo to Windsor
Waterloo to Woking
Woking to Portsmouth
Woking to Southampton
Yeovil to Exeter

EASTERN MAIN LINES
Barking to Southend
Ely to Kings Lynn
Ely to Norwich
Fenchurch Street to Barking
Ipswich to Saxmundham
Liverpool Street to Ilford
Saxmundham to Yarmouth
Tilbury Loop

WESTERN MAIN LINES
Didcot to Swindon
Ealing to Slough
Exeter to Newton Abbot
Newton Abbot to Plymouth
Newbury to Westbury
Paddington to Ealing
Paddington to Princes Risborough
Plymouth to St. Austell
Princes Risborough to Banbury
Reading to Didcot
Slough to Newbury
St. Austell to Penzance
Taunton to Exeter
Westbury to Taunton

MIDLAND MAIN LINES
Euston to Harrow & Wealdstone
St. Pancras to St. Albans

COUNTRY RAILWAY ROUTES
Abergavenny to Merthyr
Andover to Southampton
Bath to Evercreech Junction
Bath Green Park to Bristol
Bournemouth to Evercreech Junction
Burnham to Evercreech Junction
Cheltenham to Andover
Croydon to East Grinstead
Didcot to Winchester
East Kent Light Railway
Fareham to Salisbury
Guildford to Redhill
Reading to Basingstoke
Reading to Guildford
Redhill to Ashford
Salisbury to Westbury
Stratford upon Avon to Cheltenham
Strood to Paddock Wood
Taunton to Barnstaple
Wenford Bridge to Fowey
Westbury to Bath
Woking to Alton
Yeovil to Dorchester

GREAT RAILWAY ERAS
Ashford from Steam to Eurostar
Clapham Junction 50 years of change
Festiniog in the Fifties
Festiniog in the Sixties
Festiniog 50 years of enterprise
Isle of Wight Lines 50 years of change
Railways to Victory 1944-46
Return to Blaenau 1970-82
SECR Centenary album
Talyllyn 50 years of change
Yeovil 50 years of change

LONDON SUBURBAN RAILWAYS
Caterham and Tattenham Corner
Charing Cross to Dartford
Clapham Jn. to Beckenham Jn.
Crystal Palace (HL) & Catford Loop
East London Line
Finsbury Park to Alexandra Palace
Holbourn Viaduct to Lewisham
Kingston and Hounslow Loops
Lewisham to Dartford
Lines around Wimbledon
London Bridge to Addiscombe
Mitcham Junction Lines
North London Line
South London Line
West Croydon to Epsom
West London Line
Willesden Junction to Richmond
Wimbledon to Beckenham
Wimbledon to Epsom

STEAMING THROUGH
Steaming through Cornwall
Steaming through the Isle of Wight
Steaming through Kent
Steaming through West Hants
Steaming through West Sussex

TRAMWAY CLASSICS
Aldgate & Stepney Tramways
Barnet & Finchley Tramways
Bath Tramways
Brighton's Tramways
Bristol's Tramways
Burton & Ashby Tramways
Camberwell & W.Norwood Tramways
Clapham & Streatham Tramw
Croydon's Tramways
Dover's Tramways
East Ham & West Ham Tramw
Edgware and Willesden Tram
Eltham & Woolwich Tramway
Embankment & Waterloo Trar
Enfield & Wood Green Tramw
Exeter & Taunton Tramways
Greenwich & Dartford Tramwa
Hammersmith & Hounslow Tr
Hampstead & Highgate Tramw
Hastings Tramways
Holborn & Finsbury Tramway
Ilford & Barking Tramways
Kingston & Wimbledon Tramw
Lewisham & Catford Tramway
Liverpool Tramways 1. Eastern F
Liverpool Tramways 2. Southern
Liverpool Tramways 3. Northern
Maidstone & Chatham Tramw
Margate to Ramsgate
North Kent Tramways
Norwich Tramways
Reading Tramways
Seaton & Eastbourne Tramway
Shepherds Bush & Uxbridge T
Southend-on-sea Tramways
Southwark & Deptford Tramwa
Stamford Hill Tramways
Twickenham & Kingston Tramw
Victoria & Lambeth Tramways
Waltham Cross & Edmonton Tr
Walthamstow & Leyton Tramw
Wandsworth & Battersea Tramw

TROLLEYBUS CLASSIC
Croydon Trolleybuses
Derby Trolleybuses
Hastings Trolleybuses
Huddersfield Trolleybuses
Maidstone Trolleybuses
Portsmouth Trolleybuses
Woolwich & Dartford Trolleybu

WATERWAY ALBUMS
Kent and East Sussex Waterway
London to Portsmouth Waterwa
West Sussex Waterways

MILITARY BOOKS
Battle over Portsmouth
Battle over Sussex 1940
Bombers over Sussex 1943-45
Bognor at War
Military Defence of West Susse
Military Signals from the South C
Secret Sussex Resistance
Surrey Home Guard

OTHER RAILWAY BOOK
Index to all Middleton Press sta
Industrial Railways of the South
South Eastern & Chatham Railw
London Chatham & Dover Railw
War on the Line (SR 1939-45)

BIOGRAPHY
Garraway Father & Son